CHEERFUL ABEYANCE

S. SCOTT

iUniverse, Inc.
New York Bloomington

Cheerful Abeyance

iUniverse books may be ordered through booksellers or by contacting:

iUniverse
1663 Liberty Drive
Bloomington, IN 47403
www.iuniverse.com
1-800-Authors (1-800-288-4677)

Because of the dynamic nature of the Internet, any Web addresses or links contained in this book may have changed since publication and may no longer be valid. The views expressed in this work are solely those of the author and do not necessarily reflect the views of the publisher, and the publisher hereby disclaims any responsibility for them.

ISBN: 978-1-4502-4865-5 (sc)
ISBN: 978-1-4502-4866-2 (ebook)

Printed in the United States of America

iUniverse rev. date: 08/12/2010

Cheerful Abeyance

Poets are the best recyclers of emotion. With their magnanimous nature they take the venomous and blissful pressures of their lives and turn them into eloquent art forms to uplift humanity.

Repeat the Beautiful

Repeat the Beautiful
The natural are beautiful
We're happy in their touch
They sing and flow
Their song of self
They never seem to rush
And we unwind to ambience
The truth that life should be
A pretty little moment Now
In spite of world's sad scene

Designed to Love

I've never doubted happiness
I've never doubted sky
Never doubted joy exists
I'll find it by and by
And longing for the beautiful
Ensconced in blackened times
Are mystery and my story
For love is my design

Trekking Along

Nature please release me
From dependent race
Human expectations
Are slavish sometimes base
The sea wants nothing from me
The stoic crane just flies
The aged redwood growing
Without my words or eyes
So I can laugh in wonder
I'm such a feckless speck
And find my freedom tender
Just being my own trek

Last Resort

The bills unpaid don't bother me
They're whimsy in my soul
The cluttered table potpourri
As I am getting old
And thoughts of joyous moments
Are now my biggest find
I improvise when glasses lost
And savory memories blind
You see I'm not a perfect sort
With twinkle in my eye
But as I'm free and happy me
What better peace of mind

Solo in the City

The cadence of the universe
I'm feeling it right now
In swing of girl her jogging gate
And rhythm of the Tao
The bending tree through lamp lit street
Skyscraper stolid still
In night contrasting bus and cars
Whose busy wheels give thrill
To me myself a solo part
But part of all that moves
Centered in some Greater Source
Yet movement in me still

Slowly

Listening and reflecting
Meditating day
It's sacred every minute
I can't throw it away
In spite of racing humans
My nature turtle bound
The wise in me
It has to see
That true is truly sound

Pacing my Love

When pain comes rushing into me
Into my open heart
I cannot run, I'm shunned and stunned
Like open wound that smarts
I know it's bleak illusion
Not dulcet sound of bird
Not brilliant glow of gloaming day
Not silver mountain lure
But in those Hades moments
When cruel world taunts my grace
My plan discreet, my patience deep
In keeping Love's own pace

The Secret Center

The early morning lover
Bids me to stay within
Creating thoughts I put to pen
Relieving me from sin
The sin of separation
When heart and mind are split
By politics of life that drain
All my dreams and whims
But I know soulful center
In early morning hours
It's always there that sacred spot
I keep it in my grin

Enough of Sad

Weary of a world that's weary
Seems my focus now on sad
Tenebrous and melancholy
Seek me out because I'm glad
But this gladness has its limits
Oh I wish for tender ear
To convey my wistful feeling
And renew my kindly cheer

How Grand to Be

Senior moments happy
When your memory's free from fray
You just remember what pops up
Not all the past array
The facts are not important
Nostalgia makes a case
And stories of your wondrous life
Fill ever-mindful space
I feel this way with no one
Yet everyone is me
And in the end I wish to say
How grand it is to be

Rapport with Goodness

My nightmares I have put to poem
So angst won't snap this heart on loan
Here for time to search my fate
My destiny it has a date
So in the space I call my life
I hope to kindly deal with strife
And lay good deeds at heaven's door
Reliving them as my rapport

Piquant Verve

My finest hour
The force of me
Into the rhyme
Which sets me free
And all good form
In lovely thing
I'll bear it out
As song to sing
How sweet the kindness
Of piquant Verve
Which settles every
Human nerve

To Trick with Grace

The infinite in all things
The beauty in each smile
The joy at dusk and daybreak
The sigh of grace my guile
It takes a bit of cunning
To change a sullen life
Sometimes a touch of folly
Can catalyze the light

Away From Them

Try to get the things you don't get
Put yourself in others' shoes
Those who only think the one thought
Are they loyal to the true
Oh that truth beyond all substance
Is the Love that keeps us free
But there're some that never get it
Folks are weary; best find a tree

Milling in Mind

So nice to be with my own self
How many can brag their self wealth
While others seem to count their bills
My mind has time to count my thrills
The little joys that bolster life
Are in my memory strong and bright
So should you see my milling hunch
Come mill with me ~ we'll make a brunch

Diaphanous Love

I wish there were more words for love
The affable and stars above
The metaphors they pale within
When passions roar and thunder sings
Intrepid heart with walking skills
I can't explain with words its thrill
But all know when that spirit hits
A hummingbird from pollen's tryst

Compassionately Airborne

Compassion I must feel within
I must care for myself
Know when invasions of my soul
Can breach me as a sin
And know when peace and silence
Is not where it should be
Put on my seat belt first I must
And first attend to me

Opine the True

Opine I do, I love the true
The genuine of vast sky blue
The summer sun, the sandy shore
The precious shells for kids galore
And thirsty men with hearty laugh
Enjoying dusk with beer on draft
The honest feel of sweat and rest
A thorough day with God in breast

A Child's Joy

I can't expect from life
That kind of ecstasy
That I knew as a child
When singing in the sea
My hands outstretched to heaven
My heart the size of sun
I wonder if all children feel
That happiness of One

Kissed by a Cricket

Kissed with sensual morning
Thunder storming rain
Lightning fire flies the sky
Pattering drops on pane
Heat of humid summer
Locust buzzing thick
Titmouse chirping in my ear
Fondling cheerful bliss

Rapture

My private joy
The lissome sound
Of waterfall in yard
A garden obbligato
With bird call sounding bard
So many sounds of nature sing
Before hot summer's daze
My eyes are moist
Within I smile
A cantor of God's praise

Interloping in the Fields of Childhood

My mind it thinks of lambent light
And bird calls by the sea
A summer breeze of fresh relief
And afternoon's high tea
Piquant life allaying wars
In hearts that feel as one
Pulling at Pandora's box
Vacation's august sun

Chiming Sea

Euphony of slapping sea
Ripples on the shore
Matutinal is my time
By mussel mounds galore
Gulls gainsaying with the breeze
My feet they crunch the shells
An inner ring ~ my heart does sing
Forever sounding bells

Words

Words they conjure up in me
The roots of my beginning
One word can calm a growling dog
Or keep in mind bird trilling
A lullaby is salve to child
For chanting monk their drilling
Simple words ignite in me
Symbols strong and thrilling

Easy Does It

No expectation for the joy
That comes to me each day
Don't try too hard or think too much
Let wisdom have Its Way
The humble plan inside me
Written on my heart
It seeps right through
Without to do
A calm and cheerful art

New Hampshire

I didn't hear the loons last night
We both were on vacation
We all were calm
The lake it too
In nature's grand elation
Silent concert all in tune
A cadence dear with Eastern moon

Forever

Perpetuity
I love the word forever
It conjures up in me
The beauty of eternal
It makes me feel the free
Of being in my gloaming day
Or swimming in the sun's kind rays
A fellowship with all the earth
The only pristine sense of worth
The fads they come and go you see
But perpetuity belongs to me.

Etiquette and Ambiance

Etiquette and ambiance meter all that's good
Put a spark of fantasy in the world of "should"
Wit can have a rhythm
Wry can have a face
Playing with absurdities can preserve the race
Delightful what a purpose!
Whimsy dreamer's arm
Picnics in our head make dear
Childhood and its charm

No Time For Ho Hums

To integrate I must relate
Is all I want to do
Find some joy midst toil and ploy
And bring it back to you
See the world connected
We all belong to Love
Where's your bliss?
Not on you list?
Go find it you ho hums

Healing

What to do with suffering
Offer it to moon
Launch it up to evening star
Smile with lover's swoon
Makes no sense the hateful
War against Oneself
Comely life not human spite
Heals our every wound

Special Glint

Some days we live on one man's glint
The sparkle from his eye
That furtive beam that we esteem
Gives us a hearty sigh
We smile with all that's in us
We need not walk a dog
To share our sprite and our delight
That's with us all the while

To Catch the Enchanted

I like the word enchanting
A glowing eye ~ a coal
Hyperbole on nothing
But brilliant vibrant Soul
Sometimes a shiny puddle
With rainbow prism sky
Can espouse our spirits
We never know just why

How It Tis

It's probably safe to say we suffer
All the troubles of mankind
We want to know each day why sadness
Inundates the happy mind
Why Love at times feels separation
From sin or any parting rift
Why Tom Sawyer's child of wonder
Turns in mind toward helpless drift
Is it important this speculation?
I don't know; that's how it is.
And now I'll stop this inane thinking
To be a part of how it tis

Vantage on Creation

I meet the empty page in morning
Realize the hand that writes
Was given as a loan from heaven
I am that vehicle of might
A strength that feels my joy as vantage
Genre of uniquely me
That genius of each one to measure
How they see Creator's tree

Celtic Magic

I think that I shall never write
A poem as lovely as the night
The night that holds a million dreams
And silver moon to tease our spleens
The bile within our very Soul
Is conjured up in darkest troll
A Merlin who reveals himself
From virgin pure and demon's Celt

Aware of Love

We live only to recover the Loving
Where Beauty of self must reside
Sometimes ensconced by the militant world
When the kindly are left outside
But the spark of each eye in wonder
The spirit of the eager child
The tears on the hero veteran
Can trigger that Love inside

Truly Alluring

The ambiance of presence
In mother is so dear
That warm and caring nature
Can bring out all sincere
That gentle scent of being
Makes all around secure
Quite a feat when gracious life
And poise prompts our allure

Do What I Can

My mind is where my gut is
The stress and hullabaloo
It used to be in my head
It's not a rare taboo
But plight of city living
When nature is ensconced
And people don't take strength from sky
They never do look up
So I'll keep hopeful balance
That's what I'll share with them
And get my self to nature
At least in mind I can

Returning

Returning to the earth right now
Returning to the sea
The awe I had in former days
Is now the awe of me
Sacredness as wrinkles spot
My thoughtful pensive ridge
That seeps between my seagull brows
And bid me cross the bridge

October Fest

Stop thinking and get into Nature
Go and romp on autumn path
Seize the color of the maple
Make it vivid aftermath
Linger in the orange sunrise
Brilliant time to start your days
Apple trees and cider measure
Fall into October ways
Cinnamon and pumpkin piquant
Grammy making pies and jam
Concord grapes, they're tart and tangent
Escapades into the Grand

Play on Dreary Day

On dreary days I like to play
With my imagination
In sylvan mind
I dream when time was there for speculation
A holiday needs no parade
Nor money there to squander
But furtive plan to seize the land
And jolly there to wander

On Line

All the pains in life are fodder
To the most creative mind
And the pain it sometimes tells us
We are too much part of brine
Lost in the fermenting process
When we're meant to stop at times
And regurgitate our wonder
Put our poetry to line

One with Autumn Color

Errant by foot in search of vibrant
Won't know until pursuit has caught
A fleeting ray on orange maple
An autumn day red sojourn sought
The scarlet rendering of nature
That rapture from a single tree
One verdant leaf pathway to color
Streaking through the veins of me

To Be

To be me
And then to see the others skirmish
I am without legs. I move
Without arms, but I labor
Still in my mind
Kneading some bread of joy
Rising, rising, rising
While others sleep.

Who Are You?

Escaping in this modern world
A cataleptic dreaming
To fight or flee this horrid speed
Requires a mystic's beaming
Behind my mask I'll take some time
Annoying those who want my mind
But I'll come back and when I do
A peevish smile will prompt your you

A Fight for Bliss

Nature never rushes me
It calls me to no end
Like child I play with all of life
Before I need defend
My character as resume'
A quantitative list
I fight the world until again
Recline in nature's bliss

Immortal Now

I write the things I wish to say
But sometimes feel no flow
And then again in nature's calm
I flow but words come slow
Immortality seems to say
My words need place in time
A book for fond review or such
A reverie for mind
But if my life I live it well
Who cares what others view
Fugacious I will flow with time
No end, forever new

Hummingbird Sage

Free of time, the hummingbird
Our hope for love and joy
She helps us celebrate the earth
Its beauty rich a ploy
Distracting us with laughter
Her antics swoop our soul
We find her grace in human race
Brightening life's grim toll

A Different Kind of Empty

It's the heaviness of people
The acne of their minds
That wearies me beyond the work
Of ordinary times
My hands are thick and calloused
But worn out in the earth
And such my joy of youth renewed
As I return to void

Summit

Behind the pain and kindness
Behind the road of sweet
Tenacious and the cunning
Must have the dreams they seek
Their road is filled with patience
Their visions sometimes bleak
But intent strong
They carry on
For mystics love their peak

Seize Delight

The time was right
I seized the dream
And put it in my pen
My furtive eye
Jumped to the sky
I flew with darling wren
No one was there
How could they care
But laughter filled my sight
My secret joy, relief itself
I wallowed in delight

The Song Must Go On

Gnawing pain distracting
From beauty I hold dear
The darkened day and sunny hour
Sometimes seem both austere
But as I see the comely
It's winsome nature strong
When I return from suffering's hold
I'll cherish it in song

Respite in the Sky

The clouds they are all similes
They look like something else
Their form and fluff create a buff
A blustery welkin self
And there you are in heaven
Firmament of some dream
Respite care, you're light as air
Vacation, and its free

The Mighty Free

As a child on granite rock
My chair to vantage sea
Ensconced in nature by myself
Indeed I did feel free
That freedom came when 'er I slipped
Away from world routine
And sometimes stayed as I escaped
To daydream of pristine
The artists are the free ones
Who give back with their sight
Reflections of their pondering
That freedom has great might

Inside Nature

The summer rain so subtle
It touches me though dry
It's water there for me to drink
And flowers that I spy
It whispers of the softness
That feeds in gentle time
All nature's thirst
I am alert
Whenever It I find

Star of the Sea

A woman stands inside the church
Her presence can be seen
Her lissome hands they hold a boat
And everyone she sees
That wooden shape, not idol
But symbol of the strength
The tender woman gives to all
In love's deporting grace

Divine Lull

My penchant is for cheerful eye
And child in chase of gull
On beach to see a toddler high
On back of Dad, in lull
A break of orchestrated life
Sea breeze upon my face
What wondrous prayer, my happy heart
To feel divine embrace

Pass the Time

Some pass the time with puzzles
In books a pleasure find
While others diplomatic chat
Fills in a space for mind
In nature some feel timeless
Errant on freedom's trail
People have their pleasant time
For me its poems I sail

Follow the Dots

The young can sense that joy in life
Away from folly's lot
The gossips and complaining world
They turn them all to dots
Those vaporize in picture books
Their ears intent to find
The fairy tales and dreams they seek
In every fun filled eye

Vital

Escape into imagination
Escaping from the ho hum world
The dreary plan of routine living
Is not the weary of my land
I roam in search of new perspective
I might not see a thing that's new
But in my mind I'm upside down cake
I see and taste a love renewed

Fluctuate to Beauty

Tune out the raucous moment
Tune in with Beauty's find
Our hearts they want to fluctuate
And take the best to mind
But sometimes winsome moment
It comes too fast and then
We savor it but strident life
Storms in our hearts again

Nebulous Real

Exhilarating joy
Does not always loom
It comes with love's magic
Transforming our gloom
Like Monk's Hood or Lupine
Transforming a field
With lilac abundance
From where comes that real?
The real of the happy
When we are a part
Of nebulous nothing
The lilt like of heart

Savor the Sage

Aversion to repeating
The words I use in poem
But penchant to repeating
Myself when I'm alone
I need not memorize my thoughts
Nor read them on a page
But when I've lost the magic muse
I've lost some sense of sage

The Worth of Me

Sapid is the morning
When all of me is fresh
Nirvana from my childhood days
Awaken to the best
Of cinnamon upon the rolls
And outside wood, that scent in nose
As I romp for miles to be
Just every sensual limb on tree
Whose fingers rise to sky and earth
That joy I feel is my own worth

Keeping Myself

It's a wonderful thing to be shackled with silence. I imagine as a monk in his cave. When extraneous world floats by me and my focus is a summary of inner plane. As in sickness when the body should stay put and excuses for its travels seem absurd. It's a pity that this want of quiet needs excuse of a malady's allure. I am happy when dumb with my speech box. I can chatter but prefer to observe. Life seems simple with this message of meditation. How terse is my body in reserve.

Away

Away from duty to love
Away from society to spontaneity
Away from machines to the natural
I am alive
Alive with Cabin Fever
My Walden Pond
I made at home
A willful time
I called my own
Arresting all my outside tasks
I shackled heart
To inside fast
And there to snooze
With memories long
Of authors deep
And morals strong
Sabbatical with me, myself
To take account of my life's wealth

Testimonial to Heart

My presence I know is felt
But I wish my feelings felt too
It's not a vain occupation
To know others feel as I do
Edematous my heart, puffy within
Swollen and feeling the blues
With the gravity of pen
And my blood there to lend
My passions in form come true

Mystical Prayer

Cosset me with kindly words
I love to feel your love
Pamper me with Spring-like days
Or dabbled skies above
Its true You are in heaven
But all around me too
My fondled heart has made You art
In everything I do

A Return to Love

The road to love and oneness
Is easier as a child
But what adult of status quo
Is loved for manner mild
The quota of life's efforts
A tally of this earth
Gives short account of sentient
As it does for fiscal worth
How strange obituary
Which reads to populace
A kind and gently human
Returned to Whole in bliss

Resource a Zen Poem

My voice it goes to heaven
In every poem and song
My hope is that the world can feel
My throbbing heart prolonged
In beat of rushing water
Or branch of brushing tree
That touches soul for that the goal
Reflecting love we see
At one point all is beauty
As mirror I can be
Not perfect course
But loving source
That self is self-less me

Those We Love

No one is forgotten
With their memory in our mind
No one dead when living still
Deep within we find
And all our goals and follies
There're theaters to our soul
As we romp through bygone days
And taste what we extol
The star that shines within us
Kept clear through all the years
Is stellar personality
In all we love so dear

Enchanting

Expect to find the happy
Suffused with light in day
A stormy face with sleeping smile
Needs prodding to awake
And stranger in the city
On busy street awaits
A ray of light from someone bright
As simple human bait
Affinity is always
Forever each man's word
Beyond the call of everyday
Enchanting us to wait

Sensing My Soul

It's hard to know what's in my soul
What lofty song my measure
It seems I rhyme with some sublime
A mystery I call pleasure
I do not know why it comes out
Or when my pen will treasure
Those words esteemed depicting dreams
Deep feelings at my center

Isy

I am an isy
Are you an isy too
Isies like to be their love
That is what they do
Mostly they are affable
Cheerful and they're cute
Not a lot of accolades
But you feel they're true

I Do for You

Are you busy with your life
Can you stop and have a bite
Do you have some time for tea
You seem to wanta flee
Well I'm sorta languorous slow
And I'm wistful on the go
But I'll always stop for you
'Cause that is what I do

Euphony

Controlling life with my own heart
Is such a happy skill
An inner kind of maintenance
A magnum opus thrill
Accomplished in competitive
Asserting my own way
Is not my kind of active love
Sweet words win hearts with praise

Punchinello

How nice to be mute
Delightful the chance
To give up loquacious
And commune with a glance
The teachers of old
Could rule with a glare
But the sage-like of sort
Share more with their stare
And the clown without words
His antics say all
His gestures tell feelings
His pathos our call

Confabulate the Pensive

Communicate to me your heart
I'll not look back for speech
Pensive talk to hinter soul
Is known to those who teach
The masters of the loving world
With simple kindness preach
The acts we do and thoughts we think
So vast the world they reach

Giving Up Nothing

The things that use to give me joy
Were neatly packed within
So when I tried to give them up
They wouldn't seem rescind
I wished to see if I could live
In abstinence and grin
But practice of that virtue love
I know would always win

Affinity

I'm a mystical maybe
Are you a mystical too
My joy near sea and ocean breeze
Has no plan It is true
No program of attachment
How can you catch the sea
But when I'm there I have no cares
The sea and breeze are me

Abulia

Abulia with mundane tasks
My head is in the clouds
My common sense is for the sky
Crepuscular my cry
And should I find my legs on land
To peregrinate I would
Into the air of lofty life
To dream away I could

Out of Sight a Work to Find

The truth it settles in the soul
Which once was open wide
Like wave on sand that covers crab
With sun we once could spy
And so the constant yearning
For memory of that find
An arduous task for any heart
That love in poet's mind

Flow

I write to relieve my passions
I love to relieve my heart
The flow outside and flow within
Is best of human art
And should I take a holiday
The flow comes with me too
That's why I smile from cheek to cheek
The sea in me ensues

Union

Flow the life ~ life the flow
You always thought you knew
Rafting trip right inside
Jazz the sound of blues
And rhythm in you as you go
In time with all you sigh
The breath entire of universe
A kiss to each you eye

Clouds

When I loose my lofty
Then I'm sad indeed
My heart has always been in clouds
And dreams are mead for me
Oh just give me some moments
When I am loose to roam
Starry sky or daybreak rise
With gloaming too I'm free

If Park Bench Could Talk

I love to repeat my memories
How fun to regurgitate the past
A tippler of sorts inebriate of course
Imbibed with the spirits that last
The best in humans is humor
We've all had our joys and our woes
But to go beyond them
And joke with a friend
The park bench has seen lots of those

Illusions

I've seen a lot of living
I've lived a lot of life
I have respect for those in pain
And those who wind up bright
I know of all the follies
Hubris is the worst
How can you grow compassion's wit
If you think you're God at first.

Practicing Mind

Bad thoughts like meditation
Can filter through our soul
But do not stymie natural flow
Unless their focused goal
The jealousies and pettiness
Which breech us from our heart
With practiced mind can evanesce
As fog uplifts we find

Wonder Softens Own Anger

Wonder softens own anger
When we must have our own will
When our intent sees just one way
Allay it with the drill
Of conjuring up a sunset
Or singing song within
Before you know you're coddling it
From madness into grin

True Colors

I'm feeling saddened by the world
My sorrow's there with all
With struggling mothers helpless wants
Or needful baby's call
The plaintive wish of beggar
To have his place and turn
The loss of something precious
The love that's not returned
Morose I'm not but sullen now
So bleeds the human heart
But flow I do with fellow kind
Though burning now it smarts

I'm Felt

I'd like to feel my poems are read
That means that I'm read too
I cannot hide behind a mask
Unless the mask's sky blue
And there between the roses
Or romping through the wood
Denizen of nature's friend
I've known and understood

Right Thinking

Creative mind a blessing
A benison of the heart
When sacredness of being
Is put to form as art
And noble thoughts take actions
As sentient wish takes hold
Right thinking takes it place on earth
And Goodness takes it toll

Natural Way

The noise of early morning
Is painful to the ear
A fish cannot leave depths of sea
Nor mystic leave breath dear
The yon and stretch to daybreak
A natural birth to day
Was not just meant for lofty minds
But human kind as way

Right Living

Repeating something wonderful
Remembering something good
Is such a pleasure to the mind
Right being as we would
And loving all encountered
Each sacred spec of light
How happy those who know the feel
Of living this world right

Be Alert

Be alert to what you wish
To wish for love an art
What to believe, in what succeed
To know the joy of heart
And craft all things around you
To sculpt from all a ploy
Until the passion bursts to form
From patient time and coy

Constantly Concocting

Dedication and commitment
Have always been for me
The thrust of personality
My character meant to be
As sculptor sculpts
As artist paints
As dreamer dreams his dreams
I'll congregate within my walls
Propitiating me

Stymied

Flailing and flagellate
Thrash my shadow's mind
Creative energy in me
Now baleful woe to find
Just when a stable income
Can allow my art
The leisure of my presence now
Is stymied in my heart

Love is Fun

To love with all commitment
Yet not to love at all
To sing out spring and capture hearts
A longing and a call
But like a river raging
That love contained by none
It flows and runs quite freely
A dance with love is fun

A Deeper Eloquence

It seems I speak in poetry
The eloquence of words
Expressions of the lofty mind
I'd always like incur
But better still those sounds of ploy
Far from testy world
Which prompt the depth of deeper love
A world we need explore

Tractable With Nature

I have to know my feelings
Don't give a fig for fact
The bird's kind trill, my greatest thrill
To stop when beauty's cast
I'm tractable with nature
Babies catch my eye
And affable on faces dear
I never cease to spy

A Different Kind

How grand those blessed with littleness
Those happy in their minds
Describing passions deep within
Not ordinary kind
While some rely on merchants
And others count their stock
The one who counts emotions strong
Has base built on a rock

Sacred Grip

How strange macabre slumber
The Poe in life prolonged
The murder of you know not what
To snuff out life how wrong
Or snatch the life of some heart
Whose open love's a gift
How sacred tender living
How noble tender grip

Divining

With open heart the world is mine
Because I am its part
Innocence my source of power
As child within I'm smart
And from that joy my life is rich
That happiness of mind
Though storms may rage and humans fail
In soul I feel divine

Everything and Nothing

Everything and nothing
A forever kind of spot
A comfort with eternity
I like that place of not
With no one there to judge me
In hands of universe
Returning to the source of life
In happiness immersed

Planting

My mind is fixed on happiness
As I roam through life
Yet worries trip my buoyant stride
Full of woes and strife
What can I do with worries
I'll work them into clay
Pulverize to soil that's rich
And plant my heart away

Be Quick

To theorize with bedlam
A lofty kind pursuit
But when its hits to temper it
With right words takes astute
The practicing of presence
The centering of mind
It should be quick to mollify
Those hearts when raging blind

Regaining Virtue's Gait

Sickness is distracting
From that state of grace
From that happiness inside
From that loving pace
Those who know the fluency
Cadence we hold high
Sense their song
Their patience strong
Regaining virtue's gait

The Sword of Love

The sword that cuts in battle
Also the sword of love
A weapon to invest the heart
That knight who rides above
Seeing clearly greed from creed
He rides his noble steed
And sears sincere as he recedes
Deep into our dreams

Different Kind of Tippler

I'm a different kind of tippler
Inebriate of love
Seducer with a heart that streaks
Vermillion hearts above
A cupid for sad seasons
With furtive sassy eyes
A double taker on the street
You'll search as sneaky spy

In Your Mind

Orison is love itself
Sung from happy heart
Benison of cheerful soul
A living kind of art
More noble than the grandest book
Or fortune's greatest mine
To stay abreast of worldliness
And keep God in your mind

The Burden of Humanity

I am not attached to worldliness
But humans taunt my goal
While nature frees and prayers they calm
There're always those on dole
There is a choice of focus
The hapless need some smiles
The burden woe the sad of soul
My blessings bare their trials

Cosmic Fun

I am looking for the laugh
Far beyond the groan
Far beyond the dismal crowd
That makes most sigh and moan
Just stack the troubles skyward
And add just one more pain
I'll split with roaring giggles
Its fun not to complain

Lighthearted

Dishabille a negligee
Disorder of the clouds
Dabbled days, sylvan ways
Lambent rays of sun
Morose the waking hours
Villains streak the air
I'll repose my happiness
With whimsy I can share

Return to Joy

Every pain should bring compassion
Every heart should know its home
Every anger be a journey
To more peaceful time alone
With this angst we call it worry
When the doom of life persists
Can we be for each a hero
Of the joy that does exist

Temporarily Insane

A darkened sense had bridged my soul
Far away from prayer
The orison on lips in morn
No more in heart of cares
The gossip of the outside world
Which use to stay at bay
Crept into me from early hours
And fear it seemed my way
Once knowing peace abounded me
The cold sweat of that time
I bore it out like bearing child
Resuming sane in mind

Toy With Joy

Vermillion, vivacity, verdure
Those words bring hope to my soul
My fervid heart wants to hug them
Or press them into a mold
It's strange how humans can fancy
Those simple whispers of joy
Which makes life grand for the thinking
And our time treasure to toy

Love Loves

For some love comes so natural
A heart with open door
A virtue broad and generous
A voice that asks no more
And when hard times have left their mark
And sullen mars their face
Deep down their heart is working hard
To care and love the race

I Will My Heart Back

My heart is yearning for the eminent man
A person of substance, a soul that is grand
That genius not present
I'd rather alone, find leisure of solace
Explore my own home
For that joy within me
It comes out with time
A stint by the ocean
A gander at rhyme
The song that is in me I will play it back
My smile again furtive my heartbeat on tract

Sad Without Tears

My soul is missing something
I use to pull from air
A miter to connection
The regal of aware
The sovereign of almighty
The special glint in eye
It's not there now
I'm dungeon's doom
But no one sees me cry

Stilly

My bowel is calm today
The morning star serene
The peace of ages rests in me
The storm now scud to sea
Ineffable the mystery
Of why Love's lost to us
But then one day that lilt-like sway
Resumes its joyous thrust

To Stoke the Soul

We write as to remember
Those poignant fervid times
The passion of one's lover
Or carefree happy sigh
The waltz of man and woman
Transcending human gait
Within our hearts that dulcet song
Is worth life's painful wait

Reclaiming Freedom

I can't remember worry
On romping fields as child
Beside the sea I sat for hours
With not a hint of guile
But affectation crept in
Obsequious took its hold
When grown I felt responsible
For curing sad my goal
But now with age awareness
The worries flee my mind
Back to the fields of memories
As childhood I refind

Concocting

It comes to me in brilliance
As words they find my pen
I scribble thoughts munificent
Relieving heart I can
But to recite them for the world
My timid soul takes flight
I wish them read but not by me
Concocting them my might

Propitiate Love

My mind was meant to play with wonder
The smallest trifle brings me joy
A word unique and used quite little
Can excite my longing soul
My tender strength was made for sad things
To brighten life I use the Sun
The affable within elicit
As love can conquer everyone

The Blossoms of Virtue

The flower blossoms for itself
It needs no one around
The heart must dance to song inside
When loving world abounds
To be aware of kindness
To notice courtesy
The elegant of mind and soul
They live sincerity

Repeating Stillness

The stillness of my womb is now
My calm is everlasting
What good to resurrect the dead
If life I'm not now casting
The art of life is poignant me
What better trick then staying free
To sigh again with morning air
And stretch to dawn with longing stare

Beginning Day

Beginning day with rooster's call
I mumble sound as baby
My poem must find its words of heart
And pen my spirit daily
How can I not be songbird first
Sing that music since my birth
And keep perspective from above
By spending days remembering love

The Call of Arenal in Costa Rica

In the morning as light hits volcano
And I realize I have been there
The hot molten sand churned inside me
I compare to the culture of care
When we're open to the beauty around us
Human hearts bud as flowers in us all
And the birds with the animals surround us
In the calm and tranquility of our call

Near Myself

I'm pained without my solitude
My vision watered down
Part of my life performing show
Like marionette or like clown
But that is not the silent me
Of essence centered dear
My sorrow dissipates with time
Alone I'm always near

Clear Memory

Reality is what I see
Reflecting on my life
Too many things my heart did hold
Riding them my strife
Now in remembrance of that time
And memories I hold dear
I see the truth of love I've lived
It's music crystal clear

Away from Bathos

What took me to my solitude
Away from those of stealth
A distance that I must respect
My privacy of wealth
That pure light that I honor
That stillness I call me
It must have space and time alone
Forever to flow free

Loosing and Finding

I'm always loosing something
And finding it again
I'm happy for some empty time
Then longing for a friend
Sometimes I'm oh so lonely
But all alone I love
Some things just prompt my soul to sing
I'm patient for that Love

Caring for Pure Life

Pure Life I have it all the time
Though sometimes it is hidden
Behind the cloud of world concerns
My heart not always singing
But there's a feel always in mind
That hears the bird and catches signs
Of love and laugher in the air
Of hummingbird I'm so aware

Comely Cry

Unhappiness with heart no feeling
When I can't soar with little wren
Or run like child beside the water
Flow with stream with yoga bend
To silhouette with palm tree gloaming
To smile with sunshine in my eye
To sigh with beauty all around me
I wait for that with comely cry

What to do with Sadness

When I'm feeling sad inside
My pleasantry comes out
To show a kindness to a friend
Is better than to shout
For beauty does surround us
Creating it when sad
Is wonderful a human trait
An accolade to tout

Alone in Stillness

To slip into a quiet place
With no one else around
To hide beside a mountain stream
Or room without a sound
A certain sacredness takes place
That calms beyond all storm
The secretness of Love Itself
I feel in stillness borne

Lingering Love

I do not love you less but more
Away from you not sad
Your qualities with distance pique
My heart with memory glad
How can I see you when too close
Or when we're tied by time
It's more important that we feel
Our love in lingering mind

Home from Costa Rica

Peace from inanity of worry
Calm after arduous night
Nightmare in dream gone with the beam
Stillness of morning with light
The highs and the lows now are different
As I trust in magnanimous sight
Perspective within
You can see in my grin
Avaricious for good cheer to bite

A Different Logic

My logic is a different sort
It comes by way of heart
It understands the sense of life
As intuition's art
And should I get degree in it
Credential would be song
A lilt-like frequency of me
A love that carries on

Easter Day

My cadence is not always rhyme
Which makes its own fine jingle
My poem a dream that lingers on
With cloud it waits to mingle
Be carried off with welkin sky
Find joy in every sparkling eye
And know the peace of love within
Collecting every happy whim

Succinctly Sad

Sadness seemed to plague my mind
Before I went to sleep
That lachrymose I didn't know
It subtlety stalked my deep
And when I reach the morning hour
I realized my grave sin
Abruptness of the day before
Prevented flow within

Phantom Foes

Phantom foes more furtive now
Creative is their terror
When once creative mind was used
With virtue to cure error
Humans can imagine heart
Imagine ways of peace
Paint a world we share as soul
True happiness we all seek

When to Flee

When to flee to fantasy
When with patience wait
What pains to bear and when to stare
The pain away from gait
Sometimes there's no place else to go
But till the soil and beat
Pound on the earth until rebirth
We welcome and we greet

Esteem Simple

When time I have is not enough
I'm eager for myself
I wish to love compassion's way
But know myself I must
So balance once again my heart
With mindless feckless dreams
Until I'm ready to come back
To simple I esteem

Good Goblins

The laundry done in middle day
Creative is my morn
The sacredness of night itself
Slips into me as gnome
Or goblin of a kindly ilk
Who prompts my silver dreams
To take the moon and stars I love
And put them in my schemes

Glowing with Life

To silhouette the day is fine
Trees don't shadow love in mind
I want the sky of newborn day
To fill my heart but not astray
To petty world of gossip's note
With hummingbird I wish to gloat
And possibility of my soul
I wish it real not pipe dream's droll
So I will take the angst of dark
And shadow box my eager heart
To reap the dream I wish and know
As firefly we're meant to glow

True Respite

This is work and this is worry
You can see them feel them too
But we're meant for better feelings
For our sultry mind renew
On the daffodils in springtime
As they panoply their slopes
Think our lives are more than ledgers
And our dreams are more then hopes

Beyond the Insipid

Love and trust beyond all justice
Bid us hope for inner wealth
Between the truths and faults of living
We can hope for happy self
And the person of fruition
From potential makes a stand
Leaving us with inspiration
To perpetuate the grand

Regaining the Fluent

My dearest self I'm not today
I need some time in nature
Compassion that I feel for all
It does not seem my major
Perhaps I long for solid space
Without my mind in stymied race
A meditation by the sea
For I am wed but first to me

Deep

Deep inside my dreams
Begird in sanctuary
I live my life aloof
In mind I'm quick to tarry
Along the curving road of trees
A path to sky and open sea
Refreshing heart so I can breathe
My song of love the love of me

Creative Hope

Sincere my hope has always been
In creative life
In times of worry humans seem
To give up that grand spice
Enthusiasm appears to wane
With the banal and the vain
But look and see you'll always spy
That speck of spirit in someone's eye

Free Within

In doom of war and rancid life
I'll wear a pleasant face
Mid saddened hearts and heavy trials
I'll calm the human pace
With simple acts of kindness
The largest storm at sea
Needs patient face as does the race
To keep our country free

Holding Pain

Ordeals and anguish I'll endure
And sublimate to song
What good to rant stentorian ills
It does not sooth their wrong
But I will hold and fondle them
This angst inside my womb
Until that love and peace aloof
Inside my heart resume

Soul Broker

No personality comes to glow
Without awareness of the soul
In all material world we find
It's there for good in balanced mind
Such a craft the life well spent
A time to use all riches lent

Calm on the Inner Front

There's a natural inclination
Of a brooding storm within
As day progresses into night
And we examine sin
Not act of true debauchery
But splits away from heart
As we let settle unaware
Those feelings sting and smart
How kind that dreams reflection
And respite time alone
We quilt again our loving strength
In silent sacred home

Hugging My Tree

I've always loved the grace in me
My fluent wistful symmetry
No matter what cacophony
I still have home my bodhi tree
But sometimes living lost they pelt
My inner strength in Life Itself
It's just that time I'll laugh with glee
I'll love the world and hug my tree

Playful Love

My high resolve
To fight with wit
When curt deploy
I'll keep a grip
And find some ploy
To trigger laugh
Don't want more moans
Lets hear some claps
It's all a show
Lets be buffoons
With world depressed
Let Love be Boon

Making Poetic Rhyme

Unremarkable chronic loving
Sounds like a good ideal
Taking trite and hackney words
Making them pleasantly real
Eloquent speech seems a lost art
But thinking uncommonly kind
Can boost the spirits of so many
Making poetic rhyme

Impressed with Poppies

Respond oh my heart
Not too soon to the pain
To the human endeavors
Of machines as inane
For my love needs its honing
In the quiet of spring
In the fields rich with poppies
In the robins that sing
And I don't need my pen
For kaleidoscope of thought
As I'm one with my prism
In the feelings I've wrought

The Flow of Natural Might

The psyche has it menu
Will have its way in time
That is if inner ear allows
That flow within it finds
The rush of calling nature
In brook that gurgles free
Or sounds of birds with morning light
Their song in lofty tree
The calling of all humans
To cadence with true life
Is knowing worth and giving birth
To talent's natural might

Anchored not Leased

I never doubted anchor
My anchor in the Source
My living life reminds me
Of joy and not remorse
But with the tedium of day
My heart sometimes can go astray
It's then I need the quiet beach
With solo me from world unleashed

Sweet

Content and cunning
Those qualities there
For the cogent of spirit
Forever aware
Of the inner agenda
And the laughter that piques
All the joys and the follies
That lie at our feet

Supple Life

Refreshed neath feather down I slept
Right into the day
How nice to feel relief from night
In time with stars a stay
The same respite I find on road
A drive into the mount
Of sylvan trees and languorous ease
My blessings there I count
I see so many strive in life
For accolades and such
For me the boon is supple life
Which I can love and touch

Epiphany

The beauty of serenity
The charm we share of soul
Is such a simple gift to give
A gift of finest gold
And could all see the shining through
Of Love intent to live
A star would shine
In each their mind
Of wise and kindly good

Respite

There is heaviness in evening
A tension in the air
That needs release by slumber
Or breeze from solo air
A time away from others
Of somnolence and peace
Not frangible with worries
But happily in sleep
A fugue like state of vision
Reminder of the child
When unattached to mammon
Our hearts could sing and smile

Strange

What I did I did for wonder
Abandoned to all other life
It seems a veil it shadowed sundered
Ensconced me from the world's cruel strife
I was born I felt in Eden
And through my days, my path it seems
Has kept a course, an artist's distance
Which few accredit but I esteem

Testimonial to Heart

My presence I know is felt
But I wish my feelings felt too
It's not a vain occupation
To know others feel as I do
Edematous my heart, puffy within
Swollen and feeling the blues
With the gravity of pen
And my blood there to lend
My passions in form come true

Sensing My Soul

It's hard to know what's in my soul
What lofty song my measure
It seems I rhyme with some sublime
A mystery I call pleasure
I do not know why it comes out
Or when my pen will treasure
Those words esteemed depicting dreams
Deep feelings at my center

Euphony

Controlling life with my own heart
Is such a happy skill
An inner kind of maintenance
A magnum opus thrill
Accomplished in competitive
Asserting my own way
Is not my kind of active love
Sweet words win hearts with praise

My Language

I studied so hard to speak language
Not knowing my language was love
A ploy in my life's occupation
Until my hand found its own glove
The fit of my words to their meter
With the meaning of life I pursued
I knew then that the language of being
Was in poetry that we spoke of the truth

Confabulate the Pensive

Communicate to me your heart
I'll not look back for speech
Pensive talk to hinter soul
Is known to those who teach
The masters of the loving world
With simple kindness preach
The acts we do and thoughts we think
So vast the world they reach

Of Awe Full

I'm sorry for the wrongful thinking
The world it seems is full of that
To know no better what a sadness
When love's potential is human path
How strange that some see so much beauty
While others are imbibed with law
It matters not what money have you
But how your heart is full of awe

Soul Broker

No personality comes to glow
Without awareness of the soul
In all material world we find
It's there for good in balanced mind
Such a craft the life well spent
A time to use all riches lent

My Heart Beats for Summer

I wish to escape to the moonlit lake
Creep to the water's edge
Alone does align me
With pleasure imbibes me
Lambent ripples now in my head
Flowing my soul those memories of old
Attached to Forever Joy
In morning I'm sober
To the beauty of clover
And my heart is perennial red

The Value of Real

Simple, spontaneous, and desireless
Qualities that make renegade
Maverick from riches you find them in ditches
Lowly those vagabonds in wait
For perspective of beauty around them
New leaves in wisteria sky
Oxalis in the meadow inspire them
And romps through the street mesmerize
Away from life's tedious measure
With eye for the genuine and real
How is it that more people are not like them
It is a question in value of the Real

Ode to a Skink

Skink you salamander spontaneous
No noise as you slink along
Seems your nerve system simple
Sincere your lizard-like song
In times when business trifles
With my calm and natural course
I too will be like you skink
And creep somewhere unexplored

The Mist of Mehood

My mehood is so special
Unique in all its bliss
Mellifluous that little fey
Who whispers me enlist
Into the great adventure
To individuate
To travel mist of wise Sanskrit
And love to recreate

Sunshine Wink

Don't take away the chimes in me
Don't whisper lines of misery
You have those words on tip of tongue
The kindly sounds that bring the sun
Applaud the day and wink with praise
That your deep eyes reflect God's gaze

Only the Poet

My ritual is for love and beauty
The habit of my waking day
Should I not feel my breath in morning
What use is practice of what I say
It's cumbersome when I don't feel It
The marvel of my bliss at play
They say that longing lasts forever
For poet is his song and way

Aware Of Love Now

To wake without agenda
To feel God's eye on earth
To know the garden Eden
For Love you put it first
Of vigilance be mindful
For heaven is right now
And tenuous the unaware
Who do not keep their vow

Above Pathos

It's heavy in the evening
Before I go to dream
So much emotion on me
It tempts my aching spleen
To conjure up some answer
Explain my pathos now
When in my sleep and with my poems
Compassion reigns as cloud

The Waking Poet

It's civil disobedience
In early morning wiles
With bird call rise
I meditate or reverie with smiles
Connecting all my feelings
To pamper before day
I linger on some memory
Or say the prayer of sage
Contented in my cadence
Not logical but sweet
Prepared for mundane drudgery
The challenge that I meet

Uncovering the Natural

It doesn't matter what you wear
The natural can shine through
With happy hearts they share their light
They dance out what they do
So we are seeing spirit
Without entrapping gown
Distractions they are free to go
Discovery does abound

Kind Reality

Uncivil and unloving conduct
Cut the heart for needless cause
When one right word composed and smiling
Can foster feelings, which bring applause
Alacrity we need it sorely
Enthusiasm speaks of grace
Kind thoughts bear fruit and seeds of loving
For this the beauty of our race

Weeds are Wonderful Sometimes

I can't find fault with dandelions
They blossom in the spring
As sidekicks to forsythia
In fields where robins sing
With stuffiness I've called them weeds
But then again they're flowers and seeds
That yellow hair adorning lawn
Then turning white with wind blows on
Reminders of the vibrant spring
A burst of light is what they bring

Dilatory

I'm dilatory, I've always been
Slow to see the morning wren
Waiting for the sun to rise
Not with clock but eager eye
It seems I am old fashion girl
On ballroom floor with happy twirl
An etiquette that's always been
Alacrity for every friend
And for those sad a flower in bloom
To sweep them up with Scottish broom
The only thing in me that's fast
Refulgent eyes I wish to catch

Children are Fun

Complaining is so boring
And gossip it's the worst
My mind it likes original
When clever thoughts have burst
It's wearisome just living
Ho hum just everyday
Please shed a beam from your own dream
Let child in you there play

The Air of Delight

Simple forms and colors
Bring me such delight
Suit my soul more than gold
Wealth that gives me might
Creatively I'm happy
Concocting something rare
No one can see the rainbow me
Perhaps it's in my air

Resuming Nature

Exhume me from abyss of life
Remove me from the strife
My gut and brain have been possessed
By some mundane harsh might
My heart it has amnesia,
Please repossess my soul
Which once knew love and happiness
As natural human goals
So nature come and take me
From digitals that lock
And help my mind close down at night
By dusk and not by clock

Righteous

You're wrong you know
You're always wrong
I'm right you know for I've a song
And when your silly logic wins
You're still a grouch and I've a grin
Correct you are in what you say
But do you feel and do you play?

Summarize Noble Thoughts

Summarize the noble thoughts
Let your morning praise
Be an ode to happiness
Invoking Love's own aid
And when the cross of pain appears
As humans suffer bane
Let it be an offering
For world and Christ's own fame

Trust in Nature

The bugleweed its purple tones
And violets in the grass
They welcome day in springtime light
And make me feel as lass
A young girl in the fields of life
Of meadows wanderlust
This is the youth of every day
No age can break that trust

Feeling Real

Exhilarate my whimsy
Bring back my peevish eye
With little bird I am absurd
And furtively I spy
Intending to be nature
And glib with all that's real
I dash outside at least with sigh
And breathe the hope I feel

Mutability

The rippling lake and I are free
As morning gives some time for ease
And heron takes its walk on lawn
That skirts the water of new dawn
Canadian geese then catch my eye
Their ducklings as a kayak ride
I feel as them a swanlike boast
On ferry sigh in water float

The Joy of Now

The clouds are still
The lake it moves
And trees between
Give dawning thrill
To virtue of that pristine me
And nobleness of morning breeze
How can I live and still record
The measure of my very score
But joy I have it for the time
I'll think no more for now is mine

In Mind

I find my home in morning
And all those times alone
When I am free to just be me
And distance lets me roam
Into the hearts of many
Without those quirks that blind
From genuine and sincere ones
That Love is in my mind

To Each Their Feel

Snapshot on my memory
Iris to my feel
The subtle world is for me real
While glitz around it steals
With sudden and too many
Why rush the interplay
The dedicated heart to life
Will not push joy away

Obsequious for Me

Too willing for the sunrise
Too eager for the light
When nature calls I am enthralled
And wander to the bright
Affinity then there simple
Sincerely in the now
I fight for speech for soul unleash
My heart it has no wall

Kaleidoscope

Kaleidoscope of memories
Blessings of insight
They prompt my soul, as I grow old
A benison of light
And as my body fades away
And I resume the earth
I'm happy for that wisdom learned
That Love has been my worth

Awaiting the Sun

It starts on the chimney
And spreads to the tree
Then that lovely lambent light
Comes rolling in on me
How welcome is that sunburst
In heart and in my mind
Until amnesia of the day
Leaves me dull and blind
But in my dreams and slumber
As I prepare and mend
I'm ready for the break of dawn
And joyous once again

Describing the Mystery

The poet seeks to summarize
His task the One envisualized
With metaphors and similes
Suggests the souls in us are free
That goodness and that love attest
To that great light of happiness
Those mystic thoughts of human care
At last bring us to be aware

Maze of Imperfection

For you to finish, for you to correct
Your feelings for poems on a page
Not part of perfection, the sense of reflection
Not critic but part of the sage
The wisdom of life is written in hearts
Sometimes misspelled and misnamed
But for genuine souls their earnestness knows
And finds what they wish from the maze

New Day

When the sun creeps into my garden
Invading again my heart's trend
To be part of the luminous maple
On grass stage with the violets I blend
War ceases for the weeds and the dandelions
Statuesque as they highlight the rays
Of God's wand as He touches all living
With the light that begins our new day

Relief

I'm writing to relieve myself
And if you like it, good
It seems emotions pile inside
Must vent them as I should
To feel my personality
And not be watered down
A poem can bind my soul I find
And help me hold my ground

Remembering Mother

The mindfulness of mother
Important to all souls
She spawns us from her body
And into life we grow
In nurturing of the spirit
Too much cannot be said
Sometimes that mother is a man
Or friend we deeply know

Emotionally Strong

Emotional dependence
Reminds me I'm not free
It takes some distance then I find
To help remember me
To feel resilient being
A deep talk with myself
Gives inner peace and me release
With my own inner wealth

Solo

It takes several days to recover
From the thinking and the pain in my gut
How huge are the feelings of emotion
And my heart seems as one open cut
But I can flee the angst that surrounds me
Not by the ear of a friend
But by the silence which enshrines me
Off by myself I can mend

Mirror Compassion

Sometimes I'd like to speak again
To someone I hold dear
A random sort who seems to pop
Into my vantage near
And though I wish my privacy
That distance I hold clear
How can I keep myself in tact
When compassion is my mirror

Alone by the Sea

I'm just so different in the world
Though I am truly me
I'm not in vogue but how is that
When nature makes all free
I can't explain my loneliness
Because no one can see
So I'll just pine upon a mound
Or look deep in the sea

At Last Honor

Honorable I like the word
It settles well on me
A virtue solid for the time
A feeling I can see
The presence and the aura
In humans of all class
Whose surety and calm of ease
That soul it always lasts

A Part Yet Separate

Sometimes I do begin a poem
With me myself and I
But then as I progress in words
My person seems to try
To be a part of we and all
Returning to Design
It seems I go from me to we
On paper then in mind

Wholly Metaphor

I'm not a holy one
But I'm a wholly one
Ideal it seems to splash on me
From the very Sun
And I can't leave its vision
A goat must eat its grass
My grass the world
My milk a poem
And metaphor my class

The Merit of Being

Everything so beautiful
When achievement is not best
When speed is fast in soaring bird
But not a human test
And excellence is beauty
In smile and graceful limb
What other merit could there be
Then living happiness

His Her Joy

The street sounds at the break of day
Cannot compare with birds at play
No trouble on the face of man
Whose spontaneity is his plan
And though he works for livelihood
His livelihood is his own worth
He's just on stage with gainful ploy
To be himself, his very joy

Wordless Poem

If you wish to hear my voice
Listen to my poems
They are the feelings of my heart
And sometimes of my soul
Some ditties universal
Some rhymes of playful thought
And sometimes-wordless poem of me
Is greatest joy I've wrought

Inside the Game

On top of the game
Is knowing to rest
Achieving too much
Is hubris at best
We can make a difference
But balance we must
Our spirit with body
That challenge our test

Thief Whenever

I'm a thief of sunshine
Seizing all that's sweet
Bee of sorts, as I cavort
Pillaging my treat
It's not a fancy practice
With rabble find the deep
Poppy in rock's crevice
While climbing mountain steep

High Minded

A mogul rides on palanquin
I'm riding also high
A paladin of lofty thoughts
Behind his eyes and mine
I wish to keep this posture safe
This eloquence of mind
So I will dream of Taj Mahal
And graceful prince I'll find

Riding the Clouds

The pretty words not in me now
They seem to scatter with the clouds
There were so many from my books
My tomes of words made strangers look
Perhaps a kite will fly me home
Then from my cloud another poem

A Keeper

The gift of joy not always there
But buried somewhere deep
It's only lost in memory
Which poet tries to keep
In kneading dreams reflecting fun
The mirror ball repeats
Our wondrous life and all those dear
Those memories we all seek

Center of Attraction

Cynosure is my own soul
Sorely missed today
Ensconced in beauty everywhere
But I don't feel its rays
Its mirror ball existence
Reflecting Love of all
I'll work and play, search the day
Regaining it my call

Ode to Samuel Peppy

I have a book of comely words
Those words record my life
Reflecting all the things I feel
In heroes of delight
A journey in grand novel
Or funny phrase from friend
Sometimes a random word on street
Gives heart back to defend
It's fair to say I'm sorrowful
But joy it pique's my life
A stellar word for most absurd
But bring egregious light

Replaying Bright Spirits

Desultory my lofty heart
A song of love my game
It seems I dream the same love
But don't say it the same
Denizen of spirits bright
In humans as their fame
How can I pen a word to that?
A poem my lone refrain

Carmine

Romantic red is all I see
I sneak into the heart as key
Unlock the light from every sun
That Plato preached in everyone
As cat slinks to an active prey
My intuition knows how to stay
And siphon nectar from essence sweet
My destiny in all I meet

Inside Butterflies

It's not an age for poets
But what age ever was?
A dalliance with feelings
To pen it poet does
And write it into meter
Draft it into song
To copy God how ludicrous
A poet's fate and cause

A Free Ride

I'll take a day not talking
Give up thinking too
Imagine me a vegetable
Or giraffe in the zoo
Above the petty noises
In clouds a misty me
What a lovely holiday
And the fare is free

Matitunal Lake

My colon sore with busy life
I brought it to the lake
It fed on rippling waters
And ate the firs landscape
My eyes piqued that sanguinity
The somnolent took their rest
While I the sneaky spectator
Let colon have its fest

To Weaken my Faults

Attenuate my stubborn tongue
Which judges and suspects
Sometimes my honesty can hurt
But patience, it reflects
An arduous hold to virtue
The dearest part of self
Can bring response to friends we love
By sharing wisdom's wealth

Give Us This Day

The bird it whistled to the day
In mutational setting
My eyes they beamed with such esteem
My daily bread a getting
Ready was my eager ear
My senses all in present gear
To eat of what was always there
With open heart and mind aware

Staying Airborne

Sigh ~ do you remember
Love it truly breaths
The deepest air of morning
The breeze at Gloaming Sea
And in this wind of memory
Transparently we cease
But stay abreast and in that rest
Inhale and exhale peace